What Does a CITIZEN Do?

What Does a Petitioner Do?

Enslow Publishing
101 W. 23rd Street
Suite 240
New York, NY 10011
USA

enslow.com

Rita Santos

Published in 2019 by Enslow Publishing, LLC.
101 W. 23rd Street, Suite 240, New York, NY 10011

Copyright © 2019 by Enslow Publishing, LLC.

Library of Congress Cataloging-in-Publication Data

Names: Santos, Rita, author.
Title: What does a petitioner do? / Rita Santos.
Description: New York : Enslow Publishing, LLC, [2019] | Series: What does a
citizen do? | Includes bibliographical references and index. | Audience: Grades
  5–8 |Identifiers: LCCN 2017055222| ISBN 9780766098695 (library bound) | ISBN
  9780766098701 (pbk.)
Subjects: LCSH: Petition, Right of—United States—Juvenile literature. | Petitions—
  United States—History—Juvenile literature.
Classification: LCC KF4780 .S26 2018 | DDC 322.40973—dc23
LC record available at https://lccn.loc.gov/2017055222

Printed in the United States of America

To Our Readers: We have done our best to make sure all website addresses in this
book were active and appropriate when we went to press. However, the author and
the publisher have no control over and assume no liability for the material available
on those websites or on any websites they may link to. Any comments or suggestions
can be sent by email to customerservice@enslow.com.

CONTENTS

The right to petition is protected by the Constitution.

Introduction

The day you were born you became a citizen. In most places in the world you become a citizen of the nation in which you were born. "Citizen" is a legal term that means someone is a member of a specific country. When people immigrate, or move from one country to another, they might choose to retain their citizenship with their country of origin as well as become a citizen of their new country. This is known as dual citizenship. But what does it mean to be a citizen? What do we owe to the communities we are born into?

Being a citizen is a big responsibility. As citizens we have a duty to participate in our government. The United States of America is a representative democracy, which means citizens vote for politicians to represent their wishes and make political decisions for them. But our job isn't done there; we owe it to our elected officials and to ourselves to be informed about the issues our politicians are discussing. For politicians to accurately represent their constituents they need to hear from the people in their communities. When something is wrong in our communities, it is our duty as citizens to alert our elected officials. This action is called petitioning.

What Does a Petitioner Do?

Politicians don't always get things right. Our Founding Fathers understood this and devised a system of government that includes checks and balances to ensure no one person or party has too much power. However, the Founding Fathers also knew this was not enough. They had just gained independence from a king who refused to listen to the petitions of ordinary people. For a government to truly work for all people, every citizen's voice must matter.

When the delegates from the first Congress of the American colonies chose to petition Parliament for representation, they could not have foreseen how the act would lead them to war and to the creation of the United States of America. In 1776, when it was time to write the constitution for what would become the new nation, the Founding Fathers chose to protect the right to petition the government in the First Amendment. They understood that without an avenue for the average citizen to address those in power, no change could happen.

A person who brings a petition is called a petitioner. A petition can refer to the kinds of petitions you have probably seen on the internet where people explain their grievances and sometimes suggest solutions and collect signatures from other citizens to show that the idea has support. A petition can also refer to a court proceeding. The First Amendment protects Americans' right to bring a lawsuit against their government.

Throughout the history of America, average citizens have used their power as petitioners to change the course of the nation for the better. From former slaves to students to soldiers, citizens from all walks of life have stepped into the streets and into courtrooms to address their government and demand change. Will you be one of those citizens, too?

Rights and Grievances

The story of America begins with petitioners. Between October 7 and October 25, 1765, representatives from several North American British colonies met at what would become known as the First Congress of the American Colonies.[1] Of the nine delegations present, six would sign a petition to King George objecting to the Stamp Act that had been levied against the colonies. The Stamp Act forced colonists to pay a tax on all printed material. Unfortunately, each colony had already applied its own taxes to such materials, causing colonists to be taxed twice. As they had no representation in Parliament, the colonists realized there was no one in England to speak for them. The Declaration of Rights and Grievances asserted the colonies' belief in no taxation without representation. This petition to Parliament outlined the colonies' desire to remain part of the British Empire and explained that the Stamp Act was harming the colonies and needed to be changed. The colonies were asking for a seat at Parliament's table. This congressional petition would be seen as the first organized political action of the American Revolution.[2]

After the British government refused to listen to the petitions of the colonies, the Declaration of Independence would announce a new nation.

Part of the First Amendment

This extralegal activity didn't sit well with Parliament; both houses refused the petition.[3] Ultimately, the refusal of the British government to answer the colonists' grievances would put the once-loyal colonies on the road to war. In 1776, when the Founding Fathers drafted the Constitution for the new nation they'd started, they knew they had to protect the act that had helped start the nation in the First Amendment.

While most people remember that the First Amendment grants the right to free speech, it actually guarantees five different rights. Along with the freedom of speech come freedom of religion, freedom of the press, the right to petition the government, and freedom to peaceably assemble. The right to petition the government for a redress of grievances is an often-overlooked right, but it's one of the most important. It guarantees every American citizen the right to demand the government fix a problem. It also ensures that citizens will not be punished for their petitions as the colonists often were by Parliament.

You're probably familiar with online petitions that ask for support or specific actions on many subjects, but this is just one kind of petition protected by the Constitution. A petition doesn't just have to be a form you sign your name on—it is considered any nonviolent legal means of encouraging or discouraging the government from taking action. Protest, picket lines, email campaigns, and letter-writing initiatives are all forms of petitions.

Legal petitions, or lawsuits against the government, are also guaranteed under the First Amendment. This right was so important

Bringing a case before the US Supreme Court is one of the most effective ways for citizens to petition their government.

to the Founding Fathers that in the original draft of the First Amendment only the rights to assemble and petition were included.[4]

As colonists, the Founding Fathers had been unable to address their government when they had serious issues. Parliament had often refused to hear petitions from non-royals and punished those who did petition it. The Declaration of Independence explains that governments work because citizens give them power. When governments stop listening to their citizens, they stop working, and it's up to citizens to change things. By including the right to petition in the First Amendment, the Founding Fathers offered citizens their most powerful tool to change the nation. The right to petition ensures that the public is able to participate in their government.[5] It gives Americans the right to ask the government—from the local city council all the way up to the president—to change something or right a wrong that has been done. Countless laws and even some constitutional amendments have been created or abolished due to the power of petitioners.

The Intolerable Acts

John Adams once described the Boston Tea Party by saying "The People should never rise, without doing something to be remembered—something notable and striking."[6] In 1773, Parliament instituted the Coercive Acts, a series of laws passed against the Massachusetts colony as punishment for the political protest known as the Boston Tea Party. Between 30 and 130 men are believed to have taken part in throwing 342 chests of tea into the harbor to protest taxation without representation.[7] Samuel Adams defended the protest as the colonists' only option to defend their rights against a government unwilling to listen. The Coercive Acts became known as the Intolerable Acts and helped unite the colonies against the crown.

Who Are Petitioners?

Petitioners are citizens just like you. They are people who have seen an injustice or inefficiency in some part of their government or community and want to change things. If you have ever signed a petition online, you were acting as a petitioner. These kinds of formal requests, usually signed by many people, are only one type of petition. In many states, for a politician to officially be placed on a ballot, he or she must petition would-be constituents and receive a certain number of signatures first. Only two groups of people

The Women's March on January 21, 2017, was an international protest aimed at President Trump's administration. Over five million people worldwide are estimated to have participated.

are not allowed to circulate petitions. South Dakota has a law prohibiting sex offenders from circulating petitions. People serving time in federal prison are also prohibited from circulating petitions; if they try to circulate a petition, they could be punished with solitary confinement. Prisoners are still able to file legal petitions.

A legal petition is a request for a judgment from the courts. It can take the form of a petitioner suing a person, corporation, or even the government for wrongdoing. A legal petition can also take the form of a writ of certiorari, which asks the Supreme Court to review the judgment of a lower court. These types of legal petitions have led to many landmark Supreme Court decisions that have changed America over the years.

One of the limits of the First Amendment is that while the government is required to hear petitions, it is not required to respond.[8] It's true that almost all Supreme Court cases begin as legal petitions; the court decides which cases it wants to hear. This can make it difficult for petitioners to have their day in court. Many people feel that written petitions are often ignored, but they are a useful tool for community organizers to show support for or dislike of causes that may otherwise be ignored. Social and political change take years to happen, which is why petitions can seem ineffective, but they are an important first step in a process that can take decades to come to fruition.

History of Petitions in America

Before the invention of mass media, petitions were a way to gauge how the public felt about different issues.[1] America at its birth was a much smaller nation, which meant that petitions were the driving force of legislation at the time. It was not uncommon for early petitioners to seek redress for a personal issue they were having—issues like debt relief, charges of breaking the Sabbath, and even requests for divorce.[2] As the nation grew, the way petitions were used by citizens began to change.

The Abolitionist Movement

One of the first groups to use the power of petitions was the abolitionist movement. In 1790, a religious sect known as the Quakers petitioned the government to abolish slavery.[3] Most notably, the petition was signed by Founding Father Benjamin Franklin, who became a vocal abolitionist late in life. Franklin had owned slaves early in his life but had come to find the practice inhumane. The petition

Before the invention of mass media, a public discussion like this antislavery meeting in Boston Common was a way to spread information and gain support for issues.

sparked a heated debate between pro-slavery congressmen and abolitionist congressmen. Unfortunately, the petition would ultimately fail. But abolitionists would not be swayed from their goals.

In 1835, the American Anti-Slavery Society (AAS) started what is thought to be the first direct mail campaign by sending abolitionist newspapers and documents to religious and civic leaders all over the nation.[4] The material was not well received in the South. In Charleston, South Carolina, a group calling themselves the

"Lynch Men," with help from the local postmaster general, burned mailbags containing the abolitionist materials.[5]

But the AAS wasn't done; it flooded Congress with petitions to abolish slavery. Congress responded in 1836 by passing a gag rule preventing debate on the topic. Many Americans in the North rightly saw the gag rule as a loss of their civil rights. This led to more support for antislavery politicians. Former president John Quincy Adams, who had been elected as the representative of Massachusetts, fought the gag rule on the grounds that it violated the First Amendment. It would take Adams until 1844 to convince Congress to rescind the rule and allow petitions about slavery once again. In 1865, after a bloody civil war and seventy-three years after the Quakers sent their first petition, President Abraham Lincoln would sign the Emancipation Proclamation, freeing the slaves.

Votes for Women

The Quakers were always a little ahead of the times socially. On July 19 and 20, 1848, a group of female Quaker social activists held the first convention for women's rights in Seneca Falls, New York. Elizabeth Cady Stanton was the only non-Quaker organizer. Stanton, along with her husband, the founder of the Republican Party, was a fierce abolitionist who understood that without the right to vote, women could not truly be represented in government.

More than three hundred women attended the convention. Against the wishes of her husband, Stanton wrote the Declaration of Sentiments. It was modeled closely after the Declaration of Independence and included a list of grievances about the treatment of women in America. The first two grievances were about women's lack of voting rights, a shocking notion for the time. The petition

Women petitioned for the right to vote for close to one hundred years before the passage of the NIneteenth Amendment.

for suffrage, or the right to vote, was fiercely debated during the convention. Some thought it was unnatural for women to vote, while others thought fighting for suffrage would hurt the movement. In the end one hundred attendees signed their name to the declaration. Newspapers denounced it as "the most shocking and unnatural event ever recorded in the history of womanity."[6] While the petition went unheard it rallied women across the growing nation to begin demanding their right to choose their own representatives. It would

Suffrage Hike

On a cold Monday morning in December 1912, two hundred women gathered at the 242nd Street subway station in the Bronx, New York. A new governor was about to be inaugurated in Albany, New York, and the marchers planned to mark the event by giving him a petition demanding women's suffrage in the state. The 170-mile (274-kilometer) journey took thirteen days of hiking in the snow to complete. Each woman carried a bag with the words "Votes for Women" on the side, full of suffragette literature, which they passed out in each town they marched through. The pamphlets encouraged other women to join the fight and petition the government for their rights.[7]

take seventy-two years of constant organizing and social agitation before women won the right to vote in 1920.

A Murder in Selma

The Civil Rights Act of 1964 ended segregation in the South, but it didn't go far enough in protecting the rights of black Americans. While blacks legally had the right to vote, many states were deliberately keeping blacks—and even poor whites—from voting by instituting laws like poll taxes or literacy tests that had to be paid or passed before one could vote.[8] These laws were also selectively enforced, which means a white voter might not be asked to pay the poll tax, but a black voter would. This type of disenfranchisement, or stealing of voting rights, was part of a deliberate effort to keep blacks from having a say in their government.

In January 1965, Dr. Martin Luther King Jr. and many other civil rights activists focused their attention on registering black voters in Selma, Alabama. On February 18, a nonviolent protestor named Jimmie Lee Jackson was beaten and shot by an Alabama state trooper during a voting rights march. Jackson died eight days later from his wounds. His murder was part of the inspiration for a series of marches from Selma to Montgomery, Alabama.[9]

Bloody Sunday

James Bevel, the director of the Selma voting rights movement, called for a march from Selma to Montgomery to give Governor George Wallace a petition asking him to protect black voters' rights and seek redress for Jackson's murder. On March 7, close to six hundred civil rights protestors led by John Lewis and Reverend Hosea Williams began their peaceful march to Montgomery.

What Does a Petitioner Do?

When they reached the Edmund Pettus Bridge, they encountered a wall of state troopers sent by Wallace with orders to "use whatever measures are necessary to prevent a march."[10]

As violence against black protestors had gone unpunished before, the state troopers had no reason to hold back when turning the marchers away. Americans watched on TV as, mere seconds after Reverend Williams asked to speak to the commanding officer, troops began pushing the nonviolent protestors back, beating them with nightsticks when they were pushed to the ground. The troopers fired tear gas at the unarmed citizens. Seventeen marchers were hospitalized for their injuries, while another fifty were treated for lesser wounds.

Dr. King would try to lead another march on March 9 only to be turned around, but on March 17 a federal judge ruled in favor of the protestors, saying, "The law is clear that the right to petition one's government for the redress of

The march on Selma marked a turning point in the civil rights movement.

grievances may be exercised in large groups...These rights may...be exercised by marching, even along public highways."[11] The activists would march for a third time.

On March 25, President Lyndon Johnson federalized the Alabama National Guard, ordering them to protect the safety of the protestors. This time the petitioners would march to the capital, where Governor Wallace's secretary finally accepted their petition.

Largely due to the media attention and the sympathy the nation felt for the marchers, President Johnson was able to pass the Voting Rights Act of 1965, which prohibited racial discrimination in voting.

Petitions That Changed America

Legal petitions have always been one of the strongest methods for civilians in America to change their government. In 1920, a group of Americans, including Helen Keller, Roger Nash Baldwin, and Crystal Eastman, formed the American Civil Liberties Union. Its mission was "to defend and preserve the individual rights and liberties guaranteed to every person in this country by the Constitution and laws of the United States."[1] The ACLU has defended numerous people in court. Here are three of the ACLU's famous victories that changed the Constitution and the nation for the better.

Rights for All

The rights of citizens don't end just because they've done something wrong. The police play an important role in our society, but because they have so much power over citizens, laws have been enacted to prevent the police from abusing their power. One such law began with a petition. Ernesto Miranda was arrested on March 16, 1963, on charges of kidnapping and sexual assault. A witness

The American Civil Liberties Union (ACLU) protects and defends the rights of American citizens by advocating for them in court or through lobbying efforts.

to the crime had remembered the license plate number of Miranda's truck, which caused the police to bring him in as a "person of interest."[2] Miranda voluntarily went to the precinct, where officers had him take part in a lineup. When it was finished, the officers, who still hadn't arrested Miranda, implied that he had been positively identified as the criminal and was under arrest, though he was not. This helped the officers convince Miranda to confess. Miranda was unaware of his right to remain silent and to have a lawyer present before he signed a confession.

In court, Miranda's lawyer argued that his rights had been violated and that his confession had been coerced because he was led to believe he was under arrest when he wasn't. Miranda was found guilty, but his lawyer petitioned the Supreme Court for a writ of certiorari, which means a request for the court to review his case. With the ACLU representing him, the Supreme Court ruled in his favor. The outcome of this case meant that police now had to inform suspects of their rights upon their arrest. The courts saw this as a way to prevent police from using intimidation tactics to force confessions from civilians.

Miranda was retried, and his confession was not allowed to be entered as evidence. While some had feared the Miranda ruling

Grassroots Lobbying

If you've ever been asked to call your local representative concerning a certain issue, you were taking part in what is known as grassroots lobbying. While direct lobbying tries to directly influence specific politicians, grassroots lobbying tries to convince the general public to speak to their representatives. Grassroots lobbying usually targets specific communities about issues that concern them directly. It is an important method for activists to gain support and raise awareness about different issues.

would interfere with police investigations, Miranda himself was once again found guilty. There has been no evidence that informing people of their Miranda rights is detrimental to police work.[3] As the ACLU knew, protecting the rights of felons also protects the rights of citizens who have been wrongly accused of crimes, like the couple they would represent in just a few years.

When Virginia Wasn't for Loving

Mildred and Richard Loving had been childhood sweethearts. When the time came to get married, there was just one problem: it was 1958, they were a mixed-race couple, and they lived in Virginia. At the time, Virginia was one of sixteen states that still had antimiscegenation laws on the books. These laws were designed to enforce racial segregation by making marriage and/or intercourse between whites and people of color illegal. These laws meant that because Richard was white and Mildred was black, they could not marry in Virginia. But the Lovings weren't going to let racist laws get in the way of their future. They traveled to Washington, DC, where interracial marriage was legal, and took their vows. They then returned home to Central Point, Virginia, to start their family.[4]

A month after their wedding, Mildred and Richard Loving were wakened by the police. The officers had received an anonymous tip that the couple had broken the state's anticohabitation laws. Mildred, who was pregnant, pointed to their marriage certificate, which hung on the wall. The couple had assumed Virginia would honor their marriage.[5] As the police put her in handcuffs, Mildred knew they had been wrong.

In court, the couple pleaded guilty and was sentenced to a one-year suspended sentence if they left the state and did not return

The marriage of Richard and Mildred Loving challenged Virginia's antimiscegenation laws.

together for a period of twenty-five years. The couple took the plea and moved away from Virginia. Returning home to visit relatives soon became a hassle as the couple wasn't allowed to travel together. Frustrated, Mildred wrote to Attorney General Robert F. Kennedy, who urged her to reach out to the American Civil Liberties Union.[6]

The ACLU filed a petition on the couple's behalf asking for the judgment to be vacated because it violated their Fourteenth Amendment rights. By the couple's fourth wedding anniversary in June of 1962, the ACLU had taken their case all the way to the Supreme Court. On June 12, the court came to the unanimous decision that antimiscegenation laws were unconstitutional and were created to promote the racist ideology of white supremacy. The court stated that:

> There is patently no legitimate overriding purpose independent of invidious racial discrimination which justifies this classification. The fact that Virginia prohibits only interracial marriages involving white persons demonstrates that the racial classifications must stand on their own justification, as measures designed to maintain White Supremacy.[7]

The Lovings and their three children returned home to Virginia, not knowing that in a mere fifty years, the legal precedent set by their marriage would clear the way for same-sex couples across the nation to gain marriage rights as well.

Love Wins

The Loving ruling allowed people of any race to marry, but couples of the same sex were still being discriminated against. After decades of petitioning by LGBTQ activists and the ACLU, the Supreme Court consolidated four cases challenging anti-same-sex marriage laws.[8] The court decided to evaluate the cases based on two questions: Does the Fourteenth Amendment require a state to license a marriage between two people of the same sex? Does the Fourteenth Amendment require a state to recognize a marriage between two people of the same sex when their marriage was lawfully licensed and performed out of state?[9]

On June 26, 2015, the court, in a 5–4 verdict, ruled in favor of same-sex couples, making same-sex marriage legal in the United States. The ruling referenced the Loving precedent almost a dozen times. Of the ruling, Justice Anthony Kennedy wrote:

> As some of the petitioners in these cases demonstrate, marriage embodies a love that may endure even past death. It would misunderstand these men and women to say they disrespect the idea of marriage. Their plea is that they do respect it, respect it so deeply that they seek to find its fulfillment for themselves. Their hope is not to be condemned to live in loneliness, excluded from one of civilization's oldest institutions. They ask for equal dignity in the eyes of the law. The Constitution grants them that right.[10]

How Petitions Are Used Today

Petitions have always been a legal, nonviolent way for people to encourage or discourage their government from a course of action. While some feel that petitions are easily ignored, activists see them as an important tool for showing community support. Raising awareness around an issue is a key role of grassroots organizers. Petitions are a fast and easy way to call attention to a problem that is being ignored by the government or mass media.[1] Many petitions do go unanswered, but some have been successful in their goals. Technical advances have made it easier than ever for people to start and sign petitions, but has this ease had a negative effect on petitioning?

Activism or Slacktivism?

With the advances of the digital age, circulating a petition has become easier than ever. Websites like Change.org or MoveOn.org allow anyone to start or sign a petition. Where petitioning used to involve a great deal of in-person organizing, with the help of social media, digital petitions can get thousands of signatures in hours. However, big changes are still slow to come from petitions

Internet petitions are an easy way for citizens to show their support for certain issues, but are they effective?

alone. This has led many people to believe petitions are a form of slacktivism.

When the term "slacktivism" was first coined in the 1990s, it was used to describe actions that could affect society on a small, often personal scale, like planting a tree or signing a petition. It was a shortening of the phrase "slacker activism."[2] It was meant to encourage young people to become involved in their communities and government in small ways. It was based on the belief that small actions can have large consequences. Planting a tree seems like a small step, but that tree will absorb 48 pounds (21 kilograms)

of carbon dioxide a year. Slacktivism acknowledged that activism takes a lot of work, but we can all contribute in some way.

In the late 2000s, the term began to be used negatively based around the idea that online organizing was ineffective. Critics think that activities like signing online petitions are only useful in tricking people into feeling like they have done something good. While petitions alone aren't usually enough to make change happen on the federal level, there's ample evidence that they work for local issues and are useful in changing negative corporate activities. One successful Change.org petition asked the internet company Square Space to remove the websites of white supremacists.[3] Another petition successfully asked Congress to allow female World War II pilots to be buried in Arlington National Cemetery alongside their fellow airmen.[4]

In 2014, the first piece of legislation was passed from an online petition.[5] In February 2013, digital rights activist Sina Khanifar started a petition on the White House website We the People asking for the ability to "unlock" cell phones. At the time, companies would "lock" cell phones so that they could only be used by a particular carrier. This meant that people could not switch carriers and continue to use their phone. Two weeks after the petition reached one hundred thousand signatures, the administration of President Barack Obama responded by urging the Federal Communications Commission and Congress to legalize cell phone unlocking. A year later, the president signed the Unlocking Consumer Choice and Wireless Competition Act into law.

We the People

In his memoir *Dreams from My Father*, President Obama wrote, "Change won't come from the top, I would say. Change will come from a mobilized grass roots." As a former community organizer, the president knew how vital it was for those in power to hear from ordinary citizens. Obama, a former constitutional law professor, understood that petitioning was an important part of the First Amendment. In an effort to make it easier for the general public to

The Death Star Petition

The right to petition the government is vital to our civil rights, but that doesn't make it immune from jokes. In November 2012, a We the People petition was started asking the government to build a Death Star, a fictional planet-destroying weapon from the movie *Star Wars: A New Hope*. In the movie, hero Luke Skywalker is able to destroy the Death Star because of a small flaw in its design. The petitioners stated that the creation of the weapon would cause economic stimulus and job creation. The White House's good-humored response denied the petition, saying, "the Administration does not support blowing up planets" and questions funding a weapon "with a fundamental flaw that can be exploited by a one-man starship."[6]

petition their government, his administration created the We the People website on September 22, 2011. It was a part of the White House website that allowed anyone to create or sign petitions. What made this website truly stand out from other online petitioning platforms was the president's promise to respond.

While petitions about criminal justice proceedings in the United States or other processes of federal government were not allowed, any petition that reached one hundred thousand signatures in a month was guaranteed a response. To encourage grassroots

President Barack Obama, seen here when he was in law school, helped create a digital petitioning service to help grassroot organizers be heard by politicians.

Under President Obama, the White House responded to 99 percent of all We the People petitions that reached the threshold for response.

organizing, petitions were required to reach 150 signatures within thirty days to be searchable on the whitehouse.gov website. To the surprise of many, President Obama kept his promise to listen to the people, and during his administration the White House responded to 99 percent of petitions that had reached the signature threshold. They did, however, refuse to respond to petitions regarding ongoing investigations. It took the Obama administration an average of 117 days to respond to petitions. At the time this book was written, President Donald Trump's administration had not yet responded to any petitions.[7]

Student Petitioners

While most political change in the United States comes from the work of adults, children have also used the right to petition to change laws, proving that no matter what your age, being a politically active citizen can have big results.

Free Speech in Schools

In 1965, against the wishes of many Americans, the President Lyndon Johnson sent troops to fight in a civil war going on in Vietnam. Many politicians believed it was imperative that the American-backed government of Vietnam not fall to the more popular communist government. Students, many of whom would be drafted to fight in the war upon turning eighteen, disagreed.

In Des Moines, Iowa, the Tinker siblings—John, Mary Beth, Hope, and Paul—along with their friend Christopher Eckhardt, decided to wear black armbands to school to protest the war and to support the recent Christmas Truce called for by Robert F. Kennedy. Upon learning of the students' plan, the principals of their schools

During the Vietnam War, student petitioners used the courts and the streets to make their voices heard.

banned the wearing of armbands. Mary Beth and Christopher were both suspended on December 16, while John was suspended the following day. Hope and Paul, who were both elementary school students, were not punished.[1]

The students returned to school after Christmas break had ended. While they were no longer wearing armbands, the trio decided to wear black clothing in protest for the remainder of the year.

What Does a Petitioner Do?

The Tinkers' parents helped them sue the school for violating their First Amendment rights. The case made it all the way to the Supreme Court, where the court ruled 7–2 in favor of the students. Justice Abe Fortas famously wrote, "It can hardly be argued that either students or teachers shed their constitutional rights to freedom of speech or expression at the schoolhouse gate."

Kids Defend the Environment

For years the scientific community has been warning people about the negative effects of climate change. Rising temperatures not only cause the polar ice caps to melt, which raises the sea level, they

The Tinker Test

The ruling in the Tinker case set a precedent that would be known as the substantial disruption test, or the Tinker Test. The court ruled that because the students' protest had not "materially and substantially inter-fere[d] with the requirements of appropriate discipline in the operation of the school,"[2] it was protected by the First Amendment. The Tinker Test, which has been applied to several other court cases between students and schools, states that as long as student speech or expression is not substantially disruptive to the class-room, it is protected.

Many people feel the need to petition the government to take action to reverse the negative effects of climate change.

also cause more numerous and severe weather events, like hurricanes. Many leaders around the globe have come together to work on reducing carbon emissions and other efforts, which science has shown will help slow the effects of climate change. In the United States, however, many politicians have preferred to pretend climate change does not exist.[3]

In 2015, twenty-one children and teens decided they were sick of doing nothing while politicians argued over the validity of proven scientific fact. They chose to sue the United States government for violating their constitutional right to life, liberty, and property and for failing to protect the public trust. The case, known as *Juliana v. US*, petitions the court to order the government to reduce carbon emissions to 350 parts per million by 2100 and form a plan to stabilize the climate system.

The public trust is a legal doctrine that says the government must protect and preserve a certain amount of natural resources, like coastal waters, for public use. The students claimed that the atmosphere is a natural resource that the government has not been protecting for the use of future generations. They believe that by promoting the use and production of fossil fuels and refusing to take the risks of greenhouse gas emissions seriously, the government is creating a "dangerous destabilizing climate system" that places the lives of future generations in danger.

To the surprise of many, attorneys for the US Justice Department did not attempt to refute the validity of climate change.[4] Instead they focused their arguments on the claim that reducing carbon emissions would not be effective in curbing climate change. Experts in climate change disagreed, and the courts did as well.

US district court judge Anne Aiken ruled in favor of the students, stating, "I have no doubt that the right to a climate system capable of sustaining human life is fundamental to a free and ordered society...a stable climate system is quite literally the foundation of society, without which there would be neither civilization nor progress."[5]

The ruling is currently being appealed, with a court date set for 2018. Many believe the case stands a good chance of making it all the way to the Supreme Court.[6]

Become a Petitioner

Petitioners are people who see something wrong in their communities and want to find solutions. You can be one, too. The first step is deciding what issues you care about. If you love animals, you might want to get involved in animal rights. Someone who wants to be a lawyer someday might be drawn to criminal justice reform. No matter what issue you're drawn to, you can probably find groups organizing around it.

Becoming a petitioner is as easy as finding a topic you care about and making sure your elected officials know your position on that topic.

What Does a Petitioner Do?

Once you've chosen what issue you want to focus on, do your research. Find out everything you can about the issue and what solutions people have already suggested. You can find petitions online and become a petitioner that way. Or you can start your own petition. Some petitioners choose to become activists, like Elizabeth Cady Stanton and Dr. Martin Luther King Jr. If you would also like to be an agent of social change, start by raising awareness about the issues you care about among your friends and family. Social media is a great way to spread petitions and share educational articles. Just make sure you research the validity of anything you choose to post.

If you come across a problem that no one seems to be trying to solve, see if you can come up with a solution. Being part of a democracy means that every citizen matters. It also means that as citizens we have a duty to constantly strive to make our communities better for all people. The Founding Fathers knew that politicians aren't perfect. Sometimes they make the wrong choices. Sometimes they are busy and fail to notice issues in the communities. When that happens, it's up to citizens to correct them or to bring issues to their attention. The right to petition gives every citizen the power to have his or her voice heard by elected officials. How will you use that right?

CHAPTER NOTES

Chapter 1: Rights and Grievances

1. Adam Newtown, "Petition Overview," First Amendment Center, October 10, 2002, http://www.firstamendmentcenter.org/petition-overview/.
2. C. A. Weslager, *The Stamp Act Congress* (Newark, DE: University of Delaware Press, 1976).
3. Ibid.
4. Adam Newtown.
5. Ibid.
6. John Adams, "Diary of John Adams," https://founders.archives.gov/documents/Adams/01-02-02-0003-0008-0001.
7. John K. Alexander, *Samuel Adams: America's Revolutionary Politician* (Lanham, MD: Rowman & Littlefield, 2002).
8. Ibid.

Chapter 2: History of Petitions in America

1. Adam Newtown, "Petition Overview," First Amendment Center, October 10, 2002, http://www.firstamendmentcenter.org/petition-overview/.
2. "Quaker Petition to Abolish the Slave Trade, Addressed to the First U.S. Congress, 1790," http://nationalhumanitiescenter.org/tserve/eighteen/ekeyinfo/midcolpetition.htm.
3. Nancy Pope, "America's First Direct Mail Campaign," Smithsonian Institute, July 29, 2010, http://postalmuseumblog.si.edu/2010/07/americas-first-direct-mail-campaign.html.
4. Ibid.
5. "Bolting Among the Ladies," *Oneida Whig*, August 1, 1848, http://senecafallscoverage.tumblr.com/post/78871482216/oneida-whig.

6. "25 Suffragettes Start Hike from New York to Albany to Push 'Cause,'" December 16, 1912, https://lewissuffragecollection.omeka. net/items/show/1339.

7. "Selma to Montgomery March," History.com, http://www.history. com/topics/black-history/selma-montgomery-march.

8. "Selma to Montgomery March (1965)," Martin Luther King Jr. and the Global Freedom Struggle, http://kingencyclopedia.stanford.edu/ encyclopedia/encyclopedia/enc_selma_to_montgomery_march/.

9. Ibid.

10. *Williams v. Wallace*, 240 F. Supp. 100, 106 (M.D. Ala. 1960).

11. *Williams v. Wallace*, 240 F. Supp. 100 (M.D. Ala. 1965).

Chapter 3: Petitions That Changed America

1. "About the ACLU," ACLU.org, https://www.aclu.org/about-aclu.

2. Michael S. Lief and H. Mitchell Caldwell, "You Have the Right to Remain Silent," *American Heritage*, August–September 2006.

3. Ibid.

4. "Mildred Loving," Biography.com, https://www.biography.com/ people/mildred-loving-5884.

5. Ibid.

6. Ibid.

7. *Loving v. Virginia*, 388 U.S. 1 (1967), https://law.justia.com/cases/ virginia/supreme-court/1966/6163-1.html.

8. Chris Geidner, "Supreme Court Will Hear Four Cases Challenging Same-Sex Marriage Bans," Buzzfeed.com, January 16, 2015, https://www.buzzfeed.com/chrisgeidner/supreme-court-will-hear-four-cases-challenging-same-sex-marr?utm_term=.fjpy0aV6v#. bmky5oEKQ

9. Ibid.

10. *Obergefell v. Hodges*, No. 14-556.

Chapter 4: How Petitions Are Used Today

1. Adam Newtown, "Petition Overview," First Amendment Center, October 10, 2002, http://www.firstamendmentcenter.org/ petition-overview/.

2. Henrik Serup Christensen, "Political Activities on the Internet: Slacktivism or Political Participation by Other Means?" *First Monday*, Volume 16, Number 2, February 7, 2011, http://firstmonday.org/ojs/index.php/fm/article/view/3336/2767.

3. "Victories," Change.org, https://www.change.org/victories.

4. Ibid.

5. Eleanor Goldberg, "Here Are 7 Petitions That Actually Moved the White House to Take Action," Huffington Post, February 25, 2014, https://www.huffingtonpost.com/2014/02/25/white-house-petitions-works_n_4848866.html.

6. Paul Shawcross, "This Isn't the Petition Response You're Looking For," Wired.com, January 1, 2013, https://www.wired.com/2013/01/white-house-death-star/.

7. Adi Robertson, "Will Donald Trump Keep the White House Petition Site Alive?" The Verge, March 22, 2017, https://www.theverge.com/2017/3/22/15022050/donald-trump-white-house-petition-we-the-people-update.

Chapter 5: Student Petitioners

1. "*Tinker v. Des Moines*—Landmark Supreme Court Ruling on Behalf of Student Expression," ACLU.org, https://www.aclu.org/other/tinker-v-des-moines-landmark-supreme-court-ruling-behalf-student-expression.

2. *Tinker v. Des Moines Indep. Cmty. Sch. Dist.*, 393 U.S. 503, 506 (1969).

3. Laura Parker, "'Biggest Case on the Planet' Pits Kids vs. Climate Change," *National Geographic*, March 17, 2017, https://news.nationalgeographic.com/2017/03/kids-sue-us-government-climate-change.

4. Ibid.

5. Ibid.

6. Ibid.

GLOSSARY

carbon emissions Carbon dioxide released into the atmosphere through natural and man-made means.

coerce To convince through means of force or threat.

constituent Someone who is part of a voting community.

detrimental Harmful.

disenfranchisement When a group of people is denied their right to vote.

extralegal An action beyond the authority of the law.

grievances Complaints.

imperative Being of great importance.

lobbying Promoting an issue to members of the government.

miscegenation A marriage or birth that involves members of different races.

petitioner Someone requesting a resolution to problems.

redress To solve or compensate for a problem.

slacktivism Small actions that can have a large impact over time.

substantial A large and significant amount.

writ of certiorari A document in which a lower court asks a higher court to review a court proceeding.

FURTHER READING

Books

Barrett, Dawson. *Teenage Rebels: Stories of Successful High School Activists, from the Little Rock 9 to the Class of Tomorrow.* Portland, OR: Microcosm Publishing, 2017.

Blackmon Lowery, Lynda. *Turning 15 on the Road to Freedom: My Story of the 1965 Selma Voting Rights March.* New York, NY: Speak, 2016.

Dodson, Angela P. *Remember the Ladies: Celebrating Those Who Fought for Freedom at the Ballot Box.* New York, NY: Center Street, 2017.

Krumsiek, Allison. *Civil Liberties: The Fight for Personal Freedom.* New York, NY: Lucent Press, 2017.

Websites

American Civil Liberties Union
www.aclu.org
An organization dedicated to protecting the rights of every American.

The First Amendment Center
www.firstamendmentcenter.org
An educational center that teaches the history and importance of the First Amendment of the US Constitution.

We the People
www.petitions.whitehouse.gov
A website that allows people to create and sign petitions addressed to the White House.

INDEX